AIRBNB

OUR FIRST

VRBO

Featuring

The

Blanchard

House

Diamond Heart Homes

The

Blanchard

House

By: Devoe Pelcher

ISBN-9781795200677

Airbnb My First VRBO

Published and Printed in the U.S.A. 2019
Devoe Pelcher

Airbnb My First VRBO is about how we entered into the Vacation Rental House Business in Dallas, TX. U.S.A.

Table of Content

AIRBNB MY FIRST VRBO

The Blanchard House

Published and Printed in the U.S.A. 2019
Devoe Pelcher

Introduction

The state is Texas, The city is Dallas, the neighborhood is Buckner Terrace, and the location is The Blanchard House. The Blanchard House came about when my brother-in-law came to Dallas for a football game between the Dallas Cowboys and the Washington Redskins. He came over to my house for dinner and began to explain about this house that the guys were staying in which they called a VRBO (Vacation Rental By Owner) that was located close to the stadium. He explained that he paid 300 dollars a night for two nights stay. The house had two bedrooms with an additional room converted from the garage. There was a grill in the backyard, towels in the restroom. He went on to explain more details about the house and mentioned that he rented the house through a site called Airbnb. I was interested because my present rental agreement with tenants that were being a little demanding all of the time and was just about to complete their two-year lease and I did not want to repeat this type of property leasing again.

In order not to sell the house, we decided to try out this rental approach. The major two phases of getting The Blanchard House up and in operation are Cosmetic and logistic. It is plain and simple as that.

Phase One

Cosmetics

When you do enter this type of arrangement; you might decide to rent a room or a complete house. A lot of you may decide to rent a room out of your home. You still may be able to gain plenty of insight from reading this book. The first thing that I had to do was to get the property to a standard that would be acceptable for a guest to have a pleasurable stay at our location. I will attempt to go through details to show you how I grew to become a Super Host and a Premier Partner. These are levels that you can achieve in your vacation rental business. Some sites place you in front of the pack when they have prospective guest come to their site. The rental sites love to give their potential guest a great first impression when visiting their sites.

The Blanchard house started out as a 3 bedroom, 2 baths, 1 game room, two car garage, and a sunroom. Our main targets were families and big groups to bring in more funds per rental. The rental rate can be variable as you wish. For me, I decided not to rent for less than two days and no more than 6 to 7 nights. I had heard of a couple that rented more days than this and the guest decided to stay for an undisclosed longer amount of time and it was difficult to remove them from the property without court hearings. The amount that I charge usually is in the amount of $295 to $545 per night depending on the demand of the area and the events that is going on in the city and how close I am to the event. I am very close to the Cotton Bowl stadium and I always get renters during our State Fair and Bowl games held in the stadium. The Blanchard House is only about three miles from the Cotton Bowl.

I would like to start by showing you how we increased the living space. Some of the first things that we decided to do to the house were to make the decision to convert the game/exercise/bedroom into a dedicated bedroom which did not have windows. So we decided to install a sun tube to bring in sunlight into the room to take the place of no windows. So far no one has complained about this room. The only concern one group mentioned that they could not find the light switch to cut that light off which in actuality was the sun. To their surprise they found out that it was not a light at all. Even at night, there will be a soft light peeking thru from the moonlight as if it was a dimmed light. That created our fourth bedroom.

For the fifth bedroom, we created it by giving up our formal dining room and built a wall between the formal living room and the dining room. That portion of the room had a window as well as the living room. So window light was not a problem. We changed the ceiling light fixture in the newly converted dining room. We placed two lamps on end tables near the couch against the newly created wall.

This is where a queen let out couch which would increase the sleeping capacity of the house by another two people. So far the game room sleeps two additional people after we placed a full-size bed in the room. The converted dining room sleeps two because of the queen sleeper couch. So now our total is 6 guests for far and we haven't talked about the other bedrooms yet. I will eventually get to 17 quest capability.

The outdoors of your property plays a very important role in a guest deciding to accept your property to stay for their vacations and other types of stays as well. The outside of the house we created a screen in porch type of living space, considering the flying pest that usually annoys people when trying to enjoying the outside. We have no smoking in the house. But we allow smoking outside, which we have placed ashtrays in this area.

There is a cigarette butt disposal tube in a covered patio area where the Bar B Q grill and an outside dining table is located for the guest to have an outdoor dining experience also at The Blanchard House. Also, the covered area leads out to a garden which is not necessary but we love gardening, so it was no problem in giving our guest what we love to see when we were outside. Which were the beautiful flowers in the summer, lush grass to walk in barefooted if desire. These are some of the things that we liked during the time that we stayed in the house. The hummingbird feeders are still in place during a bird show for the few people get a chance to visit the house during the season that the birds are migrating thru Texas.

The lawn has a nice St. Augustine grass that is deep green in the summer and an even golden brown color that is nice to the eye. You will be surprised how many people haven't seen a nice manicured lawn, where they can pull off their shore and desire to just walk thru the thick grass. The backyard was fenced to increase the guest privacy and give them a sense of a retreat like feeling that they can just sit back in the screened in porch.

The guests are able to sit and relax on the cushioned outdoor furniture set with coffee and end tables with ashtrays if needed. They have another option to relax and forget about their trouble in the seated outdoor night lighted lawn or at the outdoor dining table set waiting and watching the food to cook on the grill to call everyone to come and get it.

The Blanchard House is centrally air-conditioned with a 5 ton Trane air conditioning system which is serviced every spring to assure its proper working during the hard hot summer days that Texas experience and semi-cold winters. The Blanchard House has extra electric fans on stands and portable heaters if needed. We keep extra blankets available for the guest also if needed. There are throws located on the couches in the den. We had the couches located in the middle of the floor. We decided to change that arrangement because after many stays we noticed that the couches would always be backed up. And close to the walls.

We would always have to be rearranged their setup into how we want the next guest to see the house when they arrive. So to solve this problem, we set all furniture such as couches and chairs against the walls and we solved that problem.

Let talk about the den right now since we mention the couches. The den has the largest big screen in the house. All bedrooms have big screen TV's for the guest entertainment. That is the one thing that guest think should be in a house even when they do not own one in their own home. The Blanchard house has internet service with Direct TV or will always have some service from some provider. This package included local and long distance telephone alone with internet and Wi-Fi.

The den has a wall type desk with rolling acrylic desk chair. This is where the internet password is kept alone with The Blanchard house guest book. A guest book is recommended to inform guest many of the things that they may ask. We have the in processing checklist as well as the out-processing checklist in that book. The guest book also has places that the guest could visit during their stay as well as local stores, pharmacies and fast food eating places close by.

The Den also has a gas fireplace which we have removed the key and a screen placed close to the opening to prevent the guest from using. We did not feel that the fireplace needed to be used, only to create another area to clean after check out. There is a small light-weighted coffee table that can be moved if necessary for a more open room feeling, which every group seems to like.

The den, as well as the other rooms, have ceiling fans which adds a way to change the room temperature away from what the air condition is set to or assist with the air conditioning of the house where there may exist pockets of spaces that are not getting the attention of the air conditioner as should be.

At this point let me mention the decorations that are located throughout The Blanchard House. The pictures, vases, flowers, also the fixtures, and dishes etc. First, we have nailed pictures and everything else that can be nailed down to the wall. It has been many times before we did this that we found pictures off of the walls. They were either bumped into by means unknown either by horseplay or accident. They were broken and had to be replaced. There was a vase that we can't find to replace that had a B on it, in the entry hallway for Blanchard. Did not notice until cleanup was almost over and we noticed some specs of glass and looked at a picture and noticed that there was a vase in the picture that was not there anymore. This brings two other points. One is insurance and the other deposits. We charge a $200-$250 deposit for damages through one site and a $59 insurance policy on another site. Sometimes it is not worth it to go through the claim procedure when it is on a few dollars for an item. So what we have done to remedy this is to get Gorilla tape and place under vases and decorations as much as possible. In addition, we nailed pictures to the wall with nails that had no heads for less visibility.

Purchase items that would look good but was not expensive that we could afford to replace with something like it if we could not find an exact match to replace. Another point here is the more that you have in the house will lead to the more items that you must maintain such as dusting and replacing and rearrangement when out of place. There have been a lot of times we had to look for things because they were out of place and even located in another room.

Going back to the bedrooms, the master bedroom has a queen size bed that will accommodate 2 people.

There is also a futon that folds out and will sleep two people. This room is where the safe closet is located. This closet has a latch and a combination lock so possibly the main quest can use to secure valuable in and lock them up for safekeeping during their stay. So far the total of people is 10.

This room has a Jack and Jill type of bathroom where both will share the tub with shower and sunroof alone with the commode. The vanities are separate with mirrors and cabinet. Only one side has a hair dryer which could be shared. All restrooms will have an amenities area that is stocked with shampoo, conditioner, lotion, shower caps, room spray, and tissue. Under the bathroom sinks are a plunger and toilet bowl scrubber. Also there is a step type lid trash can. All trash cans through the house and outside will have a liner in them; it makes for easier trash pickups throughout the house during cleaning.

The shower curtains are the type where you can view out the top portion while the bottom part you cannot. This gives the guest a sense of security while showering in your home. Not necessary but a scale is in two of the bathrooms.

The Blanchard House bedroom 2 has a twin trundle bed set. This trundle bed slides out and is kept maintain with a fitted sheet and cover sheet on it while stowed. The bed like all of them throughout the house has double pillows, which is a new standard that is graded during your guest review of your place. This room also has a fold away crib with crib linen in place when we know an infant is coming to stay. This crib can be folded up and stored and an air mattress could be placed there for an additional bed.

The air mattress that we have are all electric and blows up high off of the floor to give more of a bed feeling rather than a low to the floor mattress feel. So that brings the total to 13. The last bedroom there is a twin set nothing special to note except for the thick rug between the beds for a soft landing for the feet when getting out of the bed and not touching a cold floor. There are rugs beside every bed landing area because there is no carpet throughout the house. There is also a dual port phone charger beside both beds alone with two electrical plugs screwed down to the table between the beds. These type of chargers are in every bedroom for the quest to charge their devices in their sleeping area. There is also one in the den for open use.

Between the den and the outside screened in porch is the first tier to the outside. This is the sunroom/game room. This room was developed for the guest to entertain themselves away from the crowd with a closable barn door to separate the room from the den. This room has a glass window and doors to view outside without experiencing and facing the outside elements. The game room is furnished with board games like checkers, chess, a table soccer game, cards for children and adults.

This room has a Pub type table with iron chairs for durability alone with two other durable iron styles chairs alone the wall for additional spectators.

The entry of the house has a red door for easily locating the house after we describe the house by saying The Blanchard House is the house with the red door. The door has a punch combination style lock that is powered by batteries. We have a backup punch code key box attached to the door with a key to the door, just in case the battery is low or out and we are not near to come and open the door. That is another grading point in their review of your location.

 Once you get into the house there is an entry table that welcomes the guest with a guest comment book for them to leave their great comments about the house.

COFFEE
is my daily
GRIND
it is how I
EXPRESSO
myself
gather
Coffee
coffee bar

The kitchen is a galley style that encompasses the coffee bar also. The coffee bar is stocked with Keurig coffee, cream, sugar, raw and cane as well as substitutes. It has a coffee cup tree which holds up to 8 cups. There are paper cups with lids, stirrers, straws, chocolate candy and packages of oatmeal for a quick breakfast. Two coffee pots, one standard and the other is the Keurig. Close by the coffee bar is a water machine that dispenses hot water as well as refrigerated and room temperature water. The kitchen has a very long table that seat 8.

There is also a high chair and a booster seat in the garage on the washer and dryer. The kitchen is stocked with pot, pans, plates, bowls, glasses, cookware, utensils, and real tableware. There is also a gas stove with double oven, microwave, toaster, blender, can opener with a set of Ginsu knives. The Blanchard Hose kitchen counter has a three well sink with a 1 horse power garbage disposal. Which is needed because when you are not there, the quest will most likely put anything in the disposal which you will like I have had to do before.

This was an important addition because we had to do just that. There was a 1/4 horsepower disposal installed a couple of years ago in which our renting tenants had the same problem of a stopped up sink resulting in a call out.

Nothing in this world move or any project stands without the operation of logistics. Saying that, I am telling you that operating The Blanchard House is an easy thing in one way and complex at other times. This is a business and not just a come to my place and leave and I will make the beds when you leave. Running this vacation rental home is a joy that my wife Cynthia and I love because we love sharing our house. We loved the house when we purchased it and have shared it throughout the years one way or another. We have enjoyed the happiness that people displayed when we shared the house with them during celebrations.

Situational Truths

An extreme imagination of mine and an optimistic mindset set me up for an extreme disappointment and a letdown that came with a realization of the real truth for the vacation rentals business. There are obstacles like any other thing in life. But all of these situations can be conquered and you can still be successful.

1. My expectation for days that I expected to rent the property in my forecast was to rent the property at least 20 days out of a month and the income that I would generate with that number. Not considering if I only rented the property out only 3 days out a certain month.

2. My expectation to wow my quest with new furniture throughout the house also was a wakeup call that will be explained later.

3. Any house needs repairs and The Blanchard House was no different

4. Operating expenses is a trick in its self, balancing what's needed and what is not.

5. The varieties of people that have visited The Blanchard House were different from my expectations. I have had a single person to rent the entire house just for him only. I have had many different age groups from 18 to elderly. We have had very clean people to people that leave everything everywhere all over the house.

One good advice here is to always check drawers, and under beds. It would not be good for your rating when your next guest find underwear or dirty socks under beds. It is just as important to look in all drawers as well. People seem to always forget something they placed in a drawer, like one guest left their medicine in a drawer.

Solutions and the Truth

1. Expectations; I had large expectations and the reality really stepped in when my initial visits were a result of the site doing me a favor and placing my rental in front of many people since I was a newbie to their site. This initial boost gave me the confidence that I thought that this would surely work. After the initial boost, there were still rental requests for a while. The next thing that I ran into, since, I was tossed into the big boy crowd. Your property gets rented now because of many factors such as;

    a. Pictures

        1. The pictures need to be good quality and describe your property in details.   Don't forget the amenities and appliances.

    b. Price

        1. Keep up with the price of your competitors. Make sure you know what is happening in your location.

c. Reviews

1. Reviews are a major selling point. People like when other people like something and tend to decide based on a pass experience.

d. Placement/Rankings

1. This is important because your rankings among your fellow host will set you closer to the top of the search engine compared to having a lower ranking. Your rank is based on a set of parameters that the website has established.

e. Amenities

1. Many people like free. A lot of things that you do you do not have to. Amenities set you above the ordinary Host and Guest see this and it helps you get a better review.

f. Shock and awe

> 1. Surprise your guest occasionally with flowers as soon as they get in. You could also leave bottle water, sodas or microwave pop corn for your guest. These are inexpensive things to shock your guest with.

g. Competition

> 1. Stay up with the completion. Look at other sites and see what other hosts are doing.

h. Location

> 1. If you have not selected a location yet. Remember the phrase; Location, Location, Location. Place rental near the action where a demand constantly exist for lodging

i. 5 star ratings and badges

> 1. Try to achieve a 5 star rating. If you know that your place has the qualities of a 5 star rental.

Be sure to ask the guess not to forget about giving you a rating and reminding them that they will not be able to see your rating of them until they rate you. They will be anxious to see how you rated them.

j. Calendar

The calendar is one of those factors use by the company to rank you. So always go to your calendar and adjust, edit, confirm. One of the most important things to do is to make sure that there is no double booking occurring on your calendar. You will pay dearly if this occurs.

k. Expenses

1. Try to refrain from buying things so fast for the property until there is extra money. This is money that you may need for next month necessities such as the utilities, repairs and replacements such as sheets, light bulbs, amenities, and maintenance items like cleaning supplies.

Being close to a beach may be another example of an advantage over your competitors during the summer.

Also, in different seasons you may find that you may have to lower the price more than you would want to. But weighed against having no one staying at your property may be a no-brainer and there are times where you may have to step in from your pockets to keep your property afloat until you began to have rentals again. In everything, the major obstacle to business is where they are located. The old adage location, location, location still plays a part, especially in the vacation rental business. If your property is located close to downtown or major sporting venues, I feel those are good locations. That is not to say that other locations are not as great. But I am just saying that, people enjoy sports and have for centuries and will go miles to attend. When they arrive, they will be looking for somewhere to stay.

Now with the internet, technology has made it a little easier for the renter to be ahead of the game and reserve our rentals to reside during their stay in our city.

The stay should be the least thing and the less stressful part of their stay and that is where we come in to play and make money while doing what we do best. "Host" Try to host thru the site at all time.

Pictures that are done professionally look so much better and seems to captivate the viewers. That is what you want o to happen. That the pictures tell such a great story on their own, that the viewer cam imagines themselves being at your properties with their group doing the things that they come to your city to do or enjoy.

Pictures that I have, I have tried to arrange them in a manner that is logical such as if someone was touring through our house. We decided to have a true profile photograph picture rather than an object, avitar or nothing at all. We felt that our prospects wanted to get a feel of who we were through our profile picture and that we were not trying to hide anything.

We felt that we wanted to be outright and visible from the initial onset of our journey of pictures that would depict our house and what we had in store for them when they selected our property for their stay.

The review system is really great if all people would just tell the truth. There is a two review system that allows both you and the guest to give each other reviews. The situation that I find a lot of times or discover is that the quest does not have a review and has stayed at rental properties before.

That is the point that I would have to use old judgment to decide if I want the person to stay or not. I could be letting good money walk out of the door. I could also be taking a chance that this is a bad rental that makes me work very hard to get the property back in order. There are hard cleans and there are easy cleans. Some guest feels like they should leave the property as good as they found it and others think that they can just have a party, trash the house and their deposit should take care of it. I prefer the fist because the deposit may take care of some of the damages. Sometimes it is not the hassle to follow through with a claim.

And as far as the cleaning fees that the guest pays, at times the cleaning fees should have been more. But sometimes you find yourself charging a higher cleaning fee and you began to have a slower renting rate. When a guest pays cleaning fees and deposits, their overall cost rises from their initial vision of what they were thinking that they were going to pay.

The review system does allow the potential guest to see you through other people eyes and view what they had to say about you and your property. It gives them an idea of whether the things that you say about you and your property are true or not.

People believe other people before they will believe you and what you have to say about your listing. Sometime when you do not have a lot of reviews; lowering the price will sometime entice them to rent your listing simply because people are looking to save money anywhere that they possibly can. Having good reviews help you also to be placed higher in the search engine. Remember what I said about the rental sites want to show off the best. The more people that select their site to acquire a rental, the more money they will make in the end.

Their rental site retrieves a portion of the rental fee as payment to help run the site, advertisements, and administration.

The amenities are what a lot of people look for in a listing. See what they can get free or what you have in your home extra that will make them decide to stay at your location. If we weren't able to cook breakfast for them, make up their beds, do laundry and bring in the morning paper for them. We did some of the least things that we co do without breaking the bank per se and still be profitable. We made sure that The Blanchard House had more than the bare necessities that one would give normally.

1. In the restroom, we made sure there was tissue and extra tissue located close by.

2. There is cable throughout the house.

3. There is hand soap located at every sink and dishwashing detergent and dishwasher liquid for the dishwasher available.

3. There are shower caps as well as shower gel, lotion, shampoo and conditioner in all restrooms.

5. We provide a highchair and a booster seat for small children.

6. A crib is provided that can fold out of the way and a tall blow-up mattress can be in its place. A good way to make a room spacious is to have a trundle bed which has a bed that pull out from under the other bed.

7. We provide charcoal, charcoal lighter for the grill.

8. There is a coffee bar as well as breakfast cereal alone with chocolate candy to snack on.

7. The Blanchard House comes equipped with dishes, pots, pans, bowls, glasses, and silverware.

8. Bedside chargers/power stations are in every room.

9. The guest has access to the high-speed internet.

10. Even the ashtrays located outside and the butt deposit is an amenity because a lot of homes will not allow smoking on the property at all.

11. The grill is also an amenity. There are some people that does not even own a grill.

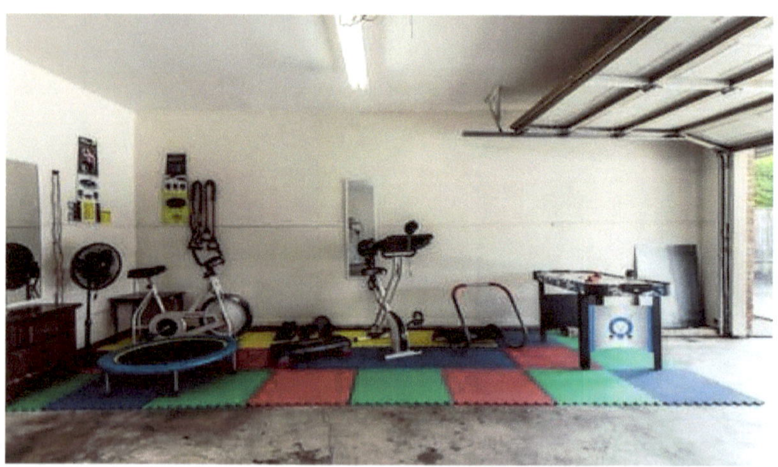

12. Games for the children to play as well as adults are in the Blanchard House game room also.

13. Having covered parking listed, garage and curb parking are well-appreciated amenities. Parking at hotels can run over $25 a night.

14. Having a Google Home or an Amazon Alexa system of some sort in the house to ask questions for directions, numbers and just to play with was a great addition to the house.

15. Having a washer and dryer is a good amenity that The Blanchard House offers.

16. Alone with this separate vanity area. There are mirrors, installed in every room for private dressing.

17. Ceiling fans can be considered an amenity as well.

18. The Blanchard House comes with a water dispenser that dispenses hot, cold and room temperature water.

19. There are clocks in every room.

20. Hair dryers are available for use in restrooms.

21. There is a toaster and microwave with available paper towels provided.

22. All closets will have hangers in them for guest to hang their cloths if they would like. We reserved three closets that we have key locks on them. One is for linen, a second for cleaning supplies and the last for maintenance and storage.

So with that said; when a person visits our vacation rental, they will get virtually everything that they may have in their home. There are so many amenities presented, that a guest would love to stay. They are looking for comfort, as if they are actually moving around in their own home room to room. So anything that I think is outside of the house itself, clean beds, something to sit on and eat at and wash up, is an amenity. Some people think that it should be a natural thing to have those things when they arrive but in actuality, those amenities came only because of competition among the host to pull a prospect in their direction to host them. This is that shock and awe aspects that wows quest and draw them to your property. If the things here, does not work to bring you, guest. I would imagine that location could be an issue as well as your pricing. This is where a person would look and evaluate if the vacation rental business is vital to their success.

Usually, these types of amenities result in getting a 5-star rating every time. There are occasions where people will just not be satisfied no matter how much you give and offer to them.

There are always people that will never be satisfied and is accustomed to more than you have to offer and think that they should be getting that level at the price that you have set for them to stay. There was even a guy who said that it was just going to be two couples at the house. Evidence indicated that there were approximately ten or more people that stayed overnight and he gave me 4 stars on value. So even when people are getting over, they are still hard to satisfy. It will take a brave and bold person with plenty of understanding that will allow some things to just roll on by. You cannot spend all of your energy on a lot of small things that you could just have let go and on to the next guest.

Phase 2 Logistics

There is nothing in this world that doesn't move or any project that stands without the operation of logistics. Saying that, I am telling you that operating The Blanchard House is an easy thing in one way and complex at other times. This is a business and not just a come to my place and leave and I will make the bed when you leave. Running this vacation rental home is a joy that my wife Cynthia and I love, because we love sharing our house. We loved the house when we purchased it and have shared it throughout the years one way or another. We have enjoyed the happiness that people displayed when we shared the house with them during celebrations.

1. City permit. Whenever you are considering renting your space. There may be rules in place that you may need to check in with your city or municipality to avoid fines. If you have fire and theft alarms, there is also a possibility that you must register these systems with the city.

2. You must also acquire the proper type of insurance for your property as well. There is a type of insurance that you will need to get in addition to your regular insurance so that you will be covered in the event of a loss.

3. A security system is needed for times that you are not at the house and there is a space of time the house will be just sitting there vacant.

4. Safety is another issue that you must pay close attention to. There must be a working smoke detector in each bedroom. Have a gas monitor as well as a glass break detector that may be included in your alarm package.

5. Deposits are necessary in my opinion because of the mishaps that may occur by accident, fun or on purpose. Be aware that too large of a deposit may defer guest from staying because this becomes part of their final bill until the trip is over and it is refunded back to them.

Situations

An extreme imagination of mine and an optimistic mindset had set me up for an extreme disappointment and a letdown that came with a realization of the real truth for the vacation rentals business. There are obstacles like any other thing in life. But all of these situations can be conquered and you will still be able to become successful.

1. My expectation for the amount of days that I expected to rent the property in my forecast was to rent the property at least 20 days out of a month. I imagined the income that I would generate with that number. Not considering if I only rented the property out only 3 days out a certain slow months.

2. My expectation to wow my quest with new furniture throughout the house also was a wakeup call that will be explained later.

3. Any house needs repairs and The Blanchard House was no different. This house was no different especially because of its age.

4. Operating expenses is a trick in its self, balancing what's needed and what is not.

5. The varieties of people that have visited The Blanchard House were different from my expectations.

Expenses

Expenses are the biggest culprits to our profits. When you own a home compared to renting a house something that someone else owns. You already know from experience when you stayed in the house there were repairs that had to be done on a regular basis as well as pop-ups. So far just in our first year, there have been pop-ups as well as guest rental caused problems and issues. Mostly, the issues have been plumbing. So always have a plumber on standby that you can call even on holidays. The holidays are mostly when you will have guests the most, so it figures that is the time when things and mishaps will happen. If the AC is not well maintained, expect to call out an air conditioner team to repair that. We try to never let pest be seen on-premise, so you will have to invest in a contractor as I do to continuously spay or spray yourself. Try not to spay right before guest will be arriving. There may be bugs or pest that may die when they are there and show up in the weirdest places for your quest to see.

That will hurt your review also. I maintain my own yard since I only have this one rental at this time. But for someone that is not able to cut grass and be on the outside for long periods of time, you must consider a lawn man to do this work for you. There is usually a going price in your area for this help. You will have to invest in light bulbs, locks, filters, batteries, tool set, air fresheners, tissue, soap and cleaning material to keep handy.

You might not be able to clean up your property when a guest leaves. You must consider finding someone that will be dependable and be there once a guest leave and have it presentable for your next guest arrival.

Be ready to replace towels and sheets and comforters and blankets. These things don't last always, especially when you wash them on a consistent basis.

Some rental hosts have the luxury of owning their home. This situation is a good one because mortgage is one thing that they don't have to concentrate on as an expense. Their concentration is totally on the utilities, miscellaneous expenses, repairs and taxes that will come around like clockwork.

One thing that we do is to use auto drafting from a debit card that the website issues as a payment card and from The Blanchard House checking account. The only issue here is to be aware when there are not enough funds in either to cover the withdrawals that will all be coming out like clockwork every month. There are months that your rentals will not cover the expenses. We have a little cushion stored away just for those times of the year. We have found out that our location is good, but not great and sometimes we experience slow rental periods, but we have decided to stay with this form of rental compared to the traditional renting which worked us after the tenant departure. We were not able to keep the property up as how we would have like too. The ending result when tenants moved: was that so much work had to be accomplished at one time before the house was livable again.

The calendar, I repeat is one of the most important items of this business to keep up with. Dare not to have a double booking occur. The penalty for that is devastating. In most of all cases, you will be responsible for paying for your overbooked guest to stay somewhere else.

If a host is utilizing, more than one rental site to book their locations. The host need to be sure to use their sync tool that will block off days on other calendars when one site has days booked. It would not hurt to double check. This portion of the site will also show you what prices that you have for what days. If you have not touched your calendar; the software will inch you to the back of the line when showing your property. The calendar will show all of your upcoming reservations date, check-in and check-out times as well.

The cleanup of the Blanchard House consists of entering the house immediately after the guest has left. We like to do this even if we do not clean up at the time. Most of the times clean up starts at this time. We try not to book someone entering the property on the same day another party is leaving. The reason that we like to enter the property immediately is that of safety and neglect. It has been times that the guest did not lock up behind them even though that is mentioned in the guest book. We have found the garage door has been left open. Unnecessary lights or TVs', heaters or fans have been left running or items still plugged up and still on.

The refrigerator doors were left cracked and not closed properly. So many situations warrant a visit to your rental since many things can occur after a departure of guests. So when cleaning began, expect to be there at least 4 - 6 hours. This time could be longer or shorter depending on how long the guest stayed to how many guests were at the property. The one most factor in this is how dirty did the guest leave the property. In every clean-up, sheets on beds need to be changed. You do not want to miss removing a dirty sheet from the bed and it just is the number one right thing to do. Trash cans must be emptied and trash removed from the house to the trash outside. Remember to set trash out on trash days to not have trash accumulate unnecessarily. We make sure all of the restrooms are cleaned after every visit. No need to explain how to clean up the restroom. Only one advice to you always and that is to be on the lookout for left behind stands of hair. That could be on the floor or in the tub. When people are at your place, they will have their eyes open and ready to see anything out of place or something there that shouldn't be. We do not dust on every visit, but we make sure that it is done often. The mirrors are

Items that will always need cleaning as well as glass entries and exit doors.

The beds after they are made and when we do not expect guest for a period of time, we cover them with plastic to prevent dust from settling on them. We always check drawers and under beds. We have often found a sock or underwear under the beds. We have found substances in drawers, that we did not know or have an idea what it was. Your next guest does not need to see these items. For sure you will hear about it on your review. Our reviews are so important to us that we cannot afford to not check for these little time-consuming details. The property is approx. 2500 square feet, so there is always a chance to miss something. That is why we work it by a system rather than just attacking it all out in an unorganized manner. There is a final checklist that we go by to see if all items are completed or looked at. I will share some of these lists in the back of the book. We have a washer and dryer as well as a dishwasher, so we have to make sure that there is nothing left in those unintentionally. And of course, all the dishes are washed and placed in the cabinets. Pot and pan placed back in their places. The yard has a schedule that it is on to be cut and maintain for a nice curb appeal as well as match the pictures.

Since we allow people to smoke, we are responsible for having clean ashtrays. We check to see if the grill has been used if so, we make sure that it is clean for the next traveler to use if they like to.

There are times when we wash our linen ourselves and other times we take them to a laundry that wash them for us and they charge by the pound. Try to wash the sheets first to remake the beds without going into your stored and folded linen you have put away. We always try to have enough linen of all categories in order to change everything while the other linen is being cleaned. By the time we finish cleaning the house the laundry is ready to be picked up and stored in the linen closet. By the way, we have three closets, that we have changed the door knobs to a privacy lock type in order to keep linen in one, supplies in another and maintenance equipment such as nails, tape, hammer, light bulbs, and small tools in another locked away from guest. We have hardwood and tile floors through the house, so there is not much need for a lot of vacuuming except the throw rugs that we have near each bed and the large rug in the den plus the sunroom. Small rugs can be shook and place back easily.

Mostly all of the floors are maintained by sweeping and mopping since there is no complete room carpet in any room. During the cleanup time we check for light bulbs that need to be changed, fire detector batteries and room plug-in deodorizers that are in need of changing or replacing. We check the coffee bar to see what need to be replenished and make sure the water dispenser has a full bottle of water.

That completes my take on the vacation rental by owner business. I truly hope that everyone that is capable do give this a try. You can always retract and do something different. Like I have said in another book of mine called "Focus" Try something and get into business for you. This is really an easy business to achieve. You have someone that collect your money, distribute the funds to you in an account. This is your home or room that is extra to you already. Make it bring extra income into your life for a small effort on your behalf. A mentor of mine told me that a millionaire does not mind doing something over and over to gain income. I will leave you with that one great thought. Think about the singers, actors and others. And all you have to do is to get that location ready for the next guest over and over again. That does not seem that bad to me to make other people money continue to flow my way. In the mildest sense, this is what they mean when you hear the term "Exchange of Wealth".

The Blanchard House Dallas

Check In

- Key box Code XXXX, Gate Codes:XXXX, Safe Closet Code XXX
- Wi-Fi code On Wall – Bluetooth: "BWA17AAXX2" / "SL MINI TOWER"
- Guest Sign-in Book Please comment on your stay/where you are from.
- To wake up Google Home, just say "Ok Google" Then speak.
- Fire Extinguisher by refrigerator
- Sunroom and Garage have a Step Down
- TV and remotes in each bedroom. Remotes are paired with its TV.
- Fireplace not for use / Den Furniture not to be moved around.
- Gas Stove / Electric Ovens
- Coffee Bar, popcorn on microwave, couple of soft drinks in refrigerator.
- Laundry Room and Garage for guest use. Button control only no remote
- Telephone and games in sunroom / exercise equipment in garage.
- Locked closets and cabinets are guest no entry zones.
- First Aid kit in main bathroom on shelf with extra tissue.
- Candles and Flashlight in coffee bar top left drawer.
- Card Table, 6' table, extra folding chairs in garage for house use only.
- Extra Linen, blanket and towels in hallway on table.
- Patios, Grill are for use, lighter and Ashtrays located in screened porch.

Check Out

The Blanchard House is a very large house with a lot of space and areas of attention. Please return property the way that you received it. This is just a small list to take in consideration when exiting the property.

- *Take all of your possessions. Look under beds, in closets, all drawers.*
- *Lock back doors to the garage and patio.*
- *Make sure gas is turned off on stove top and that the oven is off. Cancel is the off button for the oven.*
- *Check that there are no running faucets upon departure inside and out.*
- *Note broken items and take pictures if you like of how you left the house.*

The Blanchard House is serious about taking care of its guest, as we hope that we have done for you. We love for everyone that comes to be able to enjoy what it has to offer with no exceptions. That is why there is a picture inventory of everything that is on the property in order to share that same experience with the next arriving guest. A walk thru will be performed after you vacate the premises to get ready for the next guest to enjoy their stay at the Blanchard House here in Dallas. We hope that everything was great enough for you to give us an amazing review as well as us giving you one.

Thanks so much for selecting the Blanchard House

Devoe Pelcher

The Blanchard House Host

The Blanchard Host
Check List for Cleaning

- o _ _ _ _ _ Change sheets after every visit.
- o _ _ _ _ _ Clean door windows.
- o _ _ _ _ _ Wash blankets and comforters after two visits.
- o _ _ _ _ _ Make up beds and cover with plastic.
- o _ _ _ _ _ Empty trash in every room and replace with new bag.
- o _ _ _ _ _ Check all drawers under beds and closet shelves
- o _ _ _ _ _ Sweep, dust and vacuum in every room after every visit.
- o _ _ _ _ _ Empty ash trays and wipe outside tables down. Sweep if needed.
- o _ _ _ _ _ Clean sunroom table top, position tables in room.
- o _ _ _ _ _ Straighten game and telephone shelf in sunroom.
- o _ _ _ _ _ Straighten up pillows, covers, desk and tables in den.
- o _ _ _ _ _ Place all remotes in front of TVs.
- o _ _ _ _ _ Lock laundry room cabinet, supply and linen closets and cabinets.
- o _ _ _ _ _ Open lock to safe room.
- o _ _ _ _ _ Change door code.
- o _ _ _ _ _ Clean stove and oven.
- o _ _ _ _ _ Clean table and position chairs.
- o _ _ _ _ _ Clean sinks.
- o _ _ _ _ _ Clean microwave.
- o _ _ _ _ _ Clean coffee pots.
- o _ _ _ _ _ Clean dishes, cups, glasses, silverware, place in cabinets.
- o _ _ _ _ _ Clean fridge and fill ice trays.
- o _ _ _ _ _ Wipe washer and dryer out and clean filter.
- o _ _ _ _ _ Clean laundry room sink.
- o _ _ _ _ _ Store mop, broom, vacuum and tables and chairs in garage.
- o _ _ _ _ _ Lock sunroom and back door to garage.
- o _ _ _ _ _ Plug in air fresheners and plug-ins.
- o _ _ _ _ _ Refill tissue with new rolls and stock extras.
- o _ _ _ _ _ Refill amenities tray. Shampoo, conditioner, lotion and bath soap.
- o _ _ _ _ _ Clean tubs and showers.
- o _ _ _ _ _ Check cleanliness of shower curtains.
- o _ _ _ _ _ Check inside toilet for blue cleaner.
- o _ _ _ _ _ Dry and Shine faucets.
- o _ _ _ _ _ Clean grill and place aluminum foil in bottom of grill.
- o _ _ _ _ _ Close blinds and pull back curtains.
- o _ _ _ _ _ Clean counter tops and fill paper towel holder
- o _ _ _ _ _ Windex Front door window

The Blanchard House Check List for Routine Maintenance

- Spray weekly for bugs.
- Clean windows once a month.
- Lawn maintenance every two weeks.
- Cut hedges monthly
- Water yard every 3 days.
- Trim trees semiannually / every 6 months.
- Termite control annually in February.
- Clean blinds and ceiling fans monthly.
- Drano drains monthly

Disclaimer

This portion is my disclaimer: That I assume no liability for any actions that you take or do during your daily day. All risk incidental or otherwise, arising from the use or misunderstanding of this information contained herein are entirely the responsibility of the reader and users of this information. Although careful precaution has been taken in the preparation of this material, I assume no responsibility for omissions or errors or assumptions, whether such assumptions, errors or omissions, result from negligence, accidents or any other cause or loses. No part of this publication may be reproduced. No parts are to be stored in a retrieval system or transmitted in any form or by any other means nor circulated in any form of binding or cover other than which it is published and without a similar condition including this condition is imposed on the subsequent purchaser without the prior permission in writing. You shall pursue no judgment toward me or anyone else concerning this material. You shall by no means use this material in a court of law for no reason. You may not duplicate, reprint or copy any parts or portions of this document for any purpose.

The Blanchard House

Published and Printed in the U.S.A. 2019
Devoe Pelcher

www.ingramcontent.com/pod-product-compliance
Lightning Source LLC
Chambersburg PA
CBHW040225240726
48664CB00001B/13